CONFLICT RESOLUTION IN THE MIDDLE EAST

Simulating a Diplomatic Negotiation Between Israel and Syria

J. Lewis Rasmussen
Robert B. Oakley

UNITED STATES
INSTITUTE OF PEACE PRESS

Washington, D.C.

United States Institute of Peace
1550 M Street, N.W.
Washington, D.C. 20005

First published 1992

Printed in the United States of America

Library of Congress Cataloging-in-Publication Data
Rasmussen, J. Lewis, 1963–
Simulating a diplomatic negotiation: conflict resolution in the Middle East/
J. Lewis Rasmussen, Robert B. Oakley.
  p. cm.
Includes bibliographical references.
ISBN 1-878379-19-4
1. Diplomatic negotiations in international disputes—Simulation games.
2. Israel—Foreign relations—Syria. 3. Syria— Foreign relations—Israel.
I. Oakley, Robert B., 1931– . II. Title.

JX4473.R37 1992   92-30410
341.5'01'1—dc20   CIP

Contents

Summary   v

Preface   vii

1. Games, Simulations, and Relations Between Nations   1
Coming to Terms   1
Historical Evolution   2
Policy Exercises and Conflict Resolution   6
Why Policy Exercises?   9

**2. Simulating a Diplomatic Dialogue:
Syrian-Israeli Direct Talks**   13
Historical Background   13
Objective and Rationale   15
Participant Selection   18
Planning and Briefing   19
Beginning Play: Phase One   22
Continuation of Play: Phase Two   28
Stopping Play   34

3. Post-Mortem   37
Lessons Learned: Reviewing Middle East Peace Prospects   37
Lessons Learned: Reviewing the Simulation Process   42
In Conclusion   48

Notes   51

References   57

Summary

In early November 1991, the United States Institute of Peace organized and conducted a four-day simulation of a diplomatic dialogue between two neighboring countries that had never had direct, official, bilateral talks. The policy exercise was designed to simulate the direct negotiations between Syrians and Israelis that would in fact be taking place shortly thereafter as a part of the Middle East peace process.

This essay presents a detailed description of that exercise, which was designed not for research or training purposes but as an experimental policy exercise with direct implications for peace-making and conflict resolution in the Middle East, particularly the linking of theory with practice. The description of the simulation itself is presented within the context of a broader discussion of simulations and their potential utility both for diplomats and for the field of conflict resolution.

The intensive simulation exercise was followed by a wrap-up roundtable discussion of Israeli-Syrian relationships and prospects for the overall Middle East peace negotiations. The participants proved to be very knowledgeable about the issues and the policies of their putative governments as well as about political and public attitudes and probable reactions to various events. All participants played their roles realistically. Simulated Israeli and Syrian delegations presented tough initial positions and faithfully adhered to their respective government's fundamental objectives in later sessions. This situation generated a dynamic that, during the initial phases, closely paralleled what reportedly occurred at roughly the same time (November 3-6) in Madrid at the actual opening plenary session as well as in subsequent sessions of the real Israeli-Syrian bilateral working group, which met in Washington between January and May 1992. Insights drawn from the simulation were provided informally to government officials responsible for the actual negotiations and were said to have been quite helpful.

Preface

The United States Institute of Peace has since its inception provided numerous grants to individuals and institutions studying various aspects of conflict and conflict resolution in the Middle East, and several of our fellows and grantees have done extensive research and writing on this subject. The Persian Gulf War and its aftermath altered the previously pessimistic conventional wisdom about the possibility of achieving a more peaceful and durable order in the Middle East. Helping the U.S. government respond to what were perceived as promising new opportunities became a major Institute priority in 1991. With the approval of Congress, in early spring 1991, the Institute established a Special Middle East Program in Peacemaking and Conflict Resolution to encompass several new activities and to relate them coherently to other ongoing projects already included in the Institute's permanent programs of grants, fellowships, and in-house research.

As one element in this special program, between April and June 1991, the Institute convened a study group of American experts to identify those diplomatic techniques that have worked or not worked in earlier rounds of Arab-Israeli diplomacy. Former U.S. ambassadors to Middle Eastern capitals, assistant secretaries of state, special envoys for Middle East negotiations, members of the National Security Council staff, a congressional committee aide, plus several scholars and current officials from the Department of State constituted this study group. The group's objective was to be neither all-encompassing nor exhaustive, but rather to summarize important lessons gleaned from past negotiating experiences—lessons particularly relevant for the U.S. initiative to revive Arab-Israeli negotiations in the wake of the 1991 Gulf War and to organize a Middle East Peace Conference.

The Institute's report, *Making Peace Among Arabs and Israelis* (Stein and Lewis, 1991), presents those lessons, detailing why various approaches and mediation techniques have succeeded or failed. The report does not focus on the issues of substance or propose a blueprint for a negotiated outcome to the Arab-Israeli conflict. Rather it emphasizes the diplomatic process—the means most likely to bring Arabs and Israelis together to negotiate and reach agreements.

In consultation with key officials from the Department of State, the Institute decided to follow up this study by examining the confluence of conflict resolution theory and practical experiences of past Middle East negotiations in conjunction with the convening of the Madrid Peace Conference on November 3, 1991. Rather than tackle the entire gamut of countries and issues, we chose to study the newly launched bilateral dialogue between the Syrians and the Israelis. This element of the peace process was the least understood, by the two participants as well as the United States and the then USSR, and was therefore potentially the most uncertain and volatile. For this reason, we accorded it top priority.

The following essay on simulated Syrian-Israeli direct negotiations is a result of this study. As with the earlier Stein-Lewis report, this study focuses on the diplomatic process, placing it within the framework of conflict resolution theory and the evolving fields of gaming and simulation. The study applies theory to a particular situation and, in so doing, moves from the general to the particular, from the theoretical to the practical. (Readers who are less interested in the development of simulation and gaming as tools of conflict resolution and more interested in the simulated discussion of substantive issues may wish to begin with chapter 2, "Simulating a Diplomatic Dialogue: Syrian-Israeli Direct Talks.")

The overall conclusion of those participating (more than twenty-five experts on the Middle East and/or conflict resolution) as well as those briefed on the exercise afterwards (including representatives of interested governments) was that the simulation exercise, as conducted, highlighted important procedural and substantive aspects of the real-world Israeli-Syrian negotiating dynamic. This example demonstrates how such realistic policy simulation exercises can make a valuable contribution to the successful practice of third-party mediation in a diplomatic negotiation between two hostile governments.

Samuel W. Lewis, President
United States Institute of Peace

1

Games, Simulations, and Relations Between Nations

Coming to Terms

Simulations and games have long been used to study probabilities of human interaction in a variety of settings. In essence, both simulations and games are behavioral models designed to allow participants and analysts to better understand perceptions of players and the social processes that guide them and, in some cases, to predict outcomes. However, the terms "simulation" and "game" are not used consistently. Sometimes they are referred to synonymously; in other instances these terms have clear demarcations. Standard, concise definitions remain elusive.

Paul Bracken, in defining games,[1] writes that they refer "to an exercise in which opposing . . . human players are confronted with a situation or problem and work out responses to the problem and to the moves of the opposing team" (1984:791-792). Winham, adopting a less competitively grounded position, comments that games "normally are an attempt to represent the *structural* aspects of human relationships (for example, conflict) in a simplified and limited model, usually one in which human participants are used" (1991:410; emphasis added). He continues by distinguishing simulations from games in that the former "attempt to present a more complete picture of a . . . situation." On the other hand, Hoffman, on Department of Defense gaming, suggests that simulations are but one type of game and argues that a "simulation does not require interacting teams, although political-military simulations do use human players" (1984:812).

We refer herein to both games and simulations. In general, however, when the term "game" is used, the connotation should be apparent with regard to how static or dynamic the exercise is. Moreover, games tend to "have formalized rules, are normally zero-sum and adversarial, and the objective is to win. Simulations are models of reality in which the variables chosen . . . are fewer than real-world" (Bloomfield, 1992). The Institute's simulation involved an interactive process that served to illustrate and inform about the dynamics and the subtleties of the negotiating process, particularly those deriving from the assumptions and general positions of the simulated national delegations. It was not con-strained by a zero-sum philosophy and attempted to present a more complete picture than would a "game." However, before describing this rather unusual exercise, it will be useful to locate it contextually in the history and more traditional use of simula-tions and games.

Historical Evolution

"Games" predate "simulations," and by far the oldest and probably the most well known exercises are war games. Brewer and Shubik, providing a brief history of war games,[2] note that chesslike games began to appear in the 1500s (1979:45-49).[3] By the mid-1600s, a more complex and realistic training device called King's Game became popular. King's Game, a board game, had thirty pieces to a side, thirteen functional specialties, and fourteen specific strate-gic rules. In the next century, two French card games, based on fortification principles and engagement situations, were used to train military students. It wasn't until 1811 that von Reisswitz, a Prussian lieutenant, developed what is now considered a "true war game." Von Reisswitz's game used a map, pieces to represent troops, two players and a referee, and a book filled with many detailed rules. By allowing players to locate themselves in a variety of real situations and terrain, this version marked a turning point in manual gaming.

In the late 1950s, Harold Guetzkow and colleagues developed what has become perhaps the most prominent example of simulation in international relations and international negotiation. The Inter-Nation Simulation (INS) broke new ground by requiring players to make foreign policy decisions based on interaction with previous moves of other players and by adding limited but dynamic input by those directing the experiments. As a very sophisticated and relatively complex model, it was thoroughly grounded in international relations theory and sought to validate or disprove existing theory. Through continued use over time, it also contributed to the building of additional theory (Guetzkow et al., 1963; Bloomfield, 1984; Winham, 1991).

During the same period, the RAND Corporation, under the guidance of Herbert Goldhamer and Hans Spier, developed and carried out four experimental rounds of a political exercise designed to teach government officials about the complexity of policy analysis and planning. Lincoln Bloomfield and colleagues at MIT continued extensive work on political exercises (POLEX) that modeled hypothetical but realistic "political-military crisis management, reflecting contemporary Cold War rivalries, military moves, and the constant threat of the use of force" (Bloomfield, 1984:783).

The simulations and games of the 1950s and the 1960s were generally focused on the perplexing issues surrounding security and deterrence in the nuclear age. The army, air force, and naval war colleges as well as the National Defense University, the Department of Defense, the Department of State, and a number of private universities and think tanks began to adopt the use of simulations for a variety of purposes. In many instances, both RAND and MIT models were employed.

Most of these exercises were free- or moderately free-form games that by the late 1960s had fallen "into decline and remained moribund throughout the 1970s." They were replaced largely by "mathematical models and closed-form simulations that had no human involvement in their operation" (Bracken, 1984:796-797).[4] This development responded to the preferences of those working in defense and security affairs; standardized procedures for data collection, coding, input, and evaluation make verification, comparison, and replication easier.

While war games and similar political-military exercises were relatively predominant from previous centuries through the first two-thirds of this century, a dramatic increase in the variety and use of simulations and games has recently occurred. Many individuals and organizations in both the public and private sectors are now using either computer-driven or manual simulations and games[5] for political, military, medical, economic, environmental, managerial, pedagogical, and other purposes, including personal pleasure. Attempting to develop one standard taxonomy, like achieving a single definition, is extremely difficult. In general however, there are four distinguishable *methodological categories* under which simulations and games are conducted: analytic models, machine simulations, interactive human-machine simulations, and free-form simulations (Brewer, 1986:458). Cunningham, presenting a typology of simulations and their uses, defines simulations as "device[s] for replacing some aspect of reality for the purposes of *experimentation, prediction, evaluation, or learning*" (1984:215; emphasis added). In effect, each of the four purposes reflects a dimension of a classificatory approach to the design and use of simulations.[6]

Successful peacemaking and simulations both require the confluence of inter- and multi-disciplinary approaches as well as the ability to communicate effectively and to understand the relationships among causal variables and the positions and perspectives of the respective parties. This prescription is, of course, not sufficient to guarantee success; it is, however, a necessary condition.

Currently, a number of agencies within the Departments of Defense and State, including the war colleges, the National Defense University, the Joint Chiefs of Staff, and the Foreign Service Institute, make regular use of simulations for purposes of both analysis and training. A number of nongovernmental institutions also conduct simulations as a regular component of diplomatic or international negotiation training. Among them are the Centre on Conflict, University of Geneva, Switzerland; the Salzburg Seminar,* Cambridge, Massachusetts, and Salzburg, Austria; the International Peace Academy, New York; the Conflict Management Group of the Harvard Negotiation Project,* Cambridge, Massachusetts; and the Processes on International Negotiation Project (PIN) of the International Institute for Applied Systems Analysis (IIASA),* Vienna, Austria. These programs tend to run free-form, educational simulations designed specifically for professional training.[7] Although they certainly pay attention to process, they are primarily concerned with outcome—did the diplomatic trainees solve the particular problem, did they come up with a solution, did they reach an agreement?

Simulations can also be used as a tool of formal education. Two such academic programs are Project ICONS,* housed at the University of Maryland's School of Government, and the Interactive Communications and Simulations program (ICS) at the University of Michigan's School of Education. Both programs run worldwide, multi-institution, interactive simulations (human-computer) on international conflict and negotiation for high school and college students.[8]

Finally, the Atlantic Council* and the Center for Strategic and International Studies (CSIS),* both in Washington, D.C., have developed and conducted high-level, policy-relevant, crisis-management simulations dealing with such diverse issues as public

---

*Denotes organizations that have received grants from the United States Institute of Peace to assist them in carrying out their work.

policy and media dimensions of corporate and environmental disasters, terrorist incidents, arms control issues, chemical weapons proliferation, intermediate nuclear forces (INF) verification, and internal conflict in Yugoslavia.

Policy Exercises and Conflict Resolution

Sociopolitical conflict is a product of a myriad of complex related factors. Consequently, in selecting the type of exercise best suited to promote increased understanding of a specific issue, better management of general relations between nations, or peaceful resolution of a particular sociopolitical conflict, one must consider a large number of approaches to peace as well as analyze the precise nature of the problem (or conflict) to be studied.

A recent United States Institute of Peace book, edited by Thompson and Jensen (1991) and drawing on the work of a variety of scholars and practitioners, investigates major approaches toward the study and resolution of international conflict, including security, deterrence and arms control, international law, diplomacy, negotiation, and what the editors call a "new approach"—conflict resolution.

Traditional thinking about international relations has long been mired in two major debates. The first argument centered on the legitimacy (accuracy) of realism versus idealism.[9] The second, which dominated the middle 1960s, saw J. David Singer, Hedley Bull, and others debate the role of quantitative analysis in international relations.[10] The age-old level-of-analysis argument spans both debates, is still a hot issue, and has permeated the conflict resolution field.

The question of whether "wars begin in the minds of men" or as a result of structural causes has clearly polarized the field.[11] The dichotomy is neither false nor inescapably rigid, as most scholars will admit to the influence of additional variables. However, differences of opinion remain as to which level of analysis provides more powerful explanations. Few scholars of conflict and its resolution have attempted to highlight the relationship between structural and individual causality.[12] For the purposes of this case study, the relationships at issue were those among human action (e.g., the psychological and behavioral dimensions of negotiating and decision-making), social institutions as structures (e.g., the interests, positions, and norms inherent to political regimes and their various agencies/departments, and those of the "international system"), and the accompanying constraints of political reality.

Diplomats are never totally free agents. They usually operate on the basis of instructions from their home governments or their delegation leaders. Such instructions are formulated according to political necessity. Yet some diplomats have greater flexibility to explore beyond the precise boundaries of their instructions because of their previous records of success or the nature of the particular negotiation. Governments also find themselves constrained by both domestic and international pressures. Frequently intra- and inter-agency government concerns weigh heavily, as do domestic political implications. Moreover, a particular strategy or outcome may not be tolerable to the domestic constituency (i.e., the public and/or political rivals), or it may not be compatible with the interests and needs of other foreign governments whose support is important to the home government.

Regardless of whether or not negotiators follow their instructions rigorously, the subjective elements of a conflict situation are also relevant. Perceptions, fears, needs, concerns, and such qualities as trust and other general orientations toward the adversary all affect the willingness to communicate and the effectiveness of that communication. After all, negotiators are human beings and thus subject to cognitive and affective influences. Finally, the objective elements in a conflict (*real* incompatible positions and objectives) are located somewhere between the larger "structural constraints" and the subjective, human proclivities (fears, anxieties, stereotypes, communication and miscommunication, and perceptual difficulties, including *perceived* incompatible positions and objectives). Consequently, the objective elements of a conflict are influenced by both structural constraints and human subjectivity. As one or more of the three dimensions changes, greater or lesser degrees of compatibility may obtain. The challenge is to consistently create compatibility.

The 1975 Sinai II agreement between Israel and Egypt provides a good example of these dynamics. Both parties were constrained by structural elements (political unwillingness or inability to make concessions), objective elements (initial intransigence on positions and interests), and subjective elements (distrust, fears, negative perceptions of each other, etc.). The United States, acting as a third party, helped demonstrate that the actual interests of each party were not necessarily incompatible and that positions could become more flexible. Once that was accomplished, the communication between the Egyptians and the Israelis improved to the point that original political constraints were sufficiently altered so that an agreement could be reached.

The constant play between human agents and their structural constraints reflects not only a healthy tension but a confrontation with daily reality about which we remain mostly unaware. Analysts and practitioners who are cognizant of the concomitant and reciprocal influences being exerted within complex sociopolitical situations will be better able to make decisions necessary to peacefully manage and resolve conflicts. As Dutton and Stumpf write: "Because of their multilevel nature, strategic formulation and implementation processes are often difficult to observe in real-life settings. A simulated context . . . provides a unique opportunity to observe the unfolding of processes at the individual and collective levels of analysis . . . [and to] acknowledge the embeddedness of social processes that create patterns of strategic interaction" (1991:151).

A simulation provides a unique way to examine the constant interchange between multiple outlooks and interests and to understand better these complex patterns of communicative interaction.

It enables one to see and actively respond to the effect of structural variables on individuals and to observe how human decisions in turn may affect the structural environment. Observing the dynamics inherent to a simulation allows us to become more aware of and understand better the effect that human actions and decisions may have on structural constraints. Isolating and testing for the effect of particular actions, decisions, or constraints can be done by constructing carefully the scenarios and informational input provided by the Control team during the exercise.

Cultural differences, such as behavioral norms, varying concepts of justice, the importance of time, and secrecy versus public disclosure, are also important.[13] The task is not only to learn when and how cultural influence is manifested, but to gain better understanding of its referents as well. A simulation can provide a framework in which to analyze the impact of cultural (and other) aspects of interaction between the objective and the subjective elements (fear, distrust, misperception etc.) as well as the cognitive (how human beings process information and make decisions).

Why Policy Exercises?

According to Burton (1969), ineffective communication is a major antecedent of conflict, and therefore its resolution must involve processes designed to improve communication. Bercovitch argues that "learning how to get parties to negotiate, learning how to to improve predictability and provide a cognitive framework for assimilating new information and questioning old attitudes, may be as important as any other aspect of conflict management [and resolution]" (1991:20). Furthermore, Bercovitch (1986) and Laue (1991) note that there is insufficient empirical work on the relationship between intervention technique and outcome. We need to learn more about how practitioners and adversaries can move successfully toward the management and resolution of conflict. As a first step, getting adversaries to agree to talk with one another can be extremely difficult. Furthermore, even when willing to talk, distinct groups can have enormous difficulty when attempting to communicate with one another.

The identification derived from being a member of one or more social groups becomes part of an individual's self-concept. Social identity (that part of an individual's self-concept derived from group membership) becomes extremely salient when the evaluative, emotional, and even ideological significance attached to or derived from the group predominates. When the interpersonal dimensions of a relationship become subordinated to intergroup dimensions, the classic situation of "US versus THEM"— complete with misperception and misattribution—predominates.[14]

Interpersonal, intergroup, and intercultural factors, as well as several levels of political constraints, clearly influence the complicated continuum of communicative dimensions in international diplomatic interaction.[15] Avoiding, mitigating, managing, and resolving conflict is anything but easy. Political reality suggests that states are not always going to cooperate with one another. Even if they are cooperative, resolution of what often appear to be incompatible interests and objectives can prove immensely difficult. States themselves do not cooperate or talk with one another; rather, international relations are built on interpersonal interactions—human representatives of states communicating with one another across interpersonal, intergroup, and intercultural dimensions. Clearly, effective communication is not sufficient for improving international relations; it is, however, necessary. And as Paul Rohrlich states: "Improving the effectiveness of communication between state representatives can only increase understanding of a counterpart's position, and while this may not necessarily increase agreement among them, certainly poor communication will hinder all progress to that end" (1987:125).

A simulation is a medium in which trained experts can observe communicative and behavioral interaction. By observing how participants communicate and barter, those involved in the policy exercise can better understand the demands and substantive limits of the negotiating process. By paying attention to the subjective elements revealed in communication between adversaries, exercise participants can identify unanticipated opportunities and test preconceived approaches for dealing with conflicting positions, interests, and objectives.[16]

A simulation can be a useful mechanism for providing a controlled environment to test and broaden our understanding of reality.[17] This presents both a theoretical and practical challenge across numerous disciplines, involving a number of variables inherent to conflict termination. Yet bridging the gap between practitioners and academics sometimes seems as difficult as resolving the conflicts themselves. The incorporation of theoretical insight into practitioner strategies is done too infrequently. Moreover, it is difficult to say definitively how effective a particular theoretical technique may be in an actual conflict resolution situation.[18]

In this regard, Brewer continues to argue that the practical and the theoretical "must be joined in systematic fashion, not treated piecemeal or in isolation" (1986:468). Brewer suggests that a particular type of free-form simulation, a "policy exercise," will meet these needs. He defines a "policy exercise" as a deliberate approach to designing a simulation where "goals and objectives are systematically clarified and strategic alternatives invented and evaluated. The exercise is a preparatory activity for effective participation in official decision processes; its outcomes are *not* official decisions" (1986:468). Moreover, as Brewer notes, such exercises "are not meant to predict, in the narrow sense of that concept, nor are they constructed to prescribe optimal decision-making behaviors. Rather, they identify and highlight many factors likely to enter into general crisis situations" (1984:807).[19]

A simulation, in effect, can be an active laboratory where assumptions underlying policy can be tested through play.[20] A structured, purposeful environment allows for certain statements to be made, positional offers floated, linkages explored and confidence-building measures exchanged that in real life, because of political, personal, and psychological constraints, are most likely beyond the realm of possibility. It does not guarantee that actual policy- and decision-making behavior would parallel precisely that of the simulation participants. However, if individuals participate with deep knowledge of the attitudes, policies, and negotiating positions of their respective governments, the results of the exercise can be useful for real policy planning and decision-making strategies.

2

Simulating a Diplomatic Dialogue: Syrian-Israeli Direct Talks

Historical Background

In an effort to study the probable course of Syrian-Israeli negotiations for resolution of their long-standing conflict, the Institute
first analyzed the basic nature of their relationship, the key elements
involved in the conflict that would require removal or alteration
for its resolution, and the participants' current attitudes toward
these elements and toward negotiations or other communication
between them relative to conflict resolution. Placing this analysis
in the context of fifty years of Arab-Israeli negotiations (Stein and
Lewis, 1991) and Syrian and Israeli agreement to attend the
Madrid Conference and then engage in direct bilateral talks, the
Institute concluded that a simulation offered the best means of
gaining the desired insights. It also decided, for reasons explained
below, to focus the simulation primarily on the likely dynamic of
the initial dialogue between Syria and Israel rather than on for-
mulae for resolving the various specific elements of their conflict.
These criteria influenced the type of simulation chosen, selection
of participants, and detailed organization of the simulation exercise so that the most realistic result could be achieved.

Unlike the case with Egypt, there had never been any direct,
official, bilateral talks between Syria and Israel. Nor had there

been, with two exceptions in 1949 and 1974, any significant indirect dialogue. The 1949 Armistice Accord between them was negotiated indirectly in Rhodes by UN Under Secretary Ralph Bunche. The 1974 Disengagement Agreement for the Golan had likewise been negotiated indirectly by U.S. Secretary of State Henry Kissinger. The latter agreement had actually been signed by the Egyptian general chairing the joint Syrian-Egyptian military delegation to the disengagement talks, because the Syrian delegate would not sign.

The four agreements signed by Egypt and Israel after the 1973 war (i.e., January 1974, September 1975, September 1978, and March 1979) were preceded by weeks of personal discussion with Israeli and Egyptian leaders by Secretary of State Henry Kissinger (1974-75) and President Jimmy Carter and Secretary of State Cyrus Vance (1977-79). Only by this means was enough mutual comprehension generated for the process of diplomatic dialogue to begin and, once begun, to achieve success. Publicly acknowledged tripartite meetings of senior U.S., Egyptian, and Israeli officials occurred in January and July 1978, making crucial contributions to the success of the Camp David Conference in September 1978. Yet, starting in 1977, intensive indirect Egyptian-Israeli dialogue through the United States was given a very important boost from periodic direct secret meetings between senior Israeli and Egyptian officials. To Israel, these were more important in assessing Egyptian intentions than were mediated messages from the United States.

However, except for Secretary Kissinger's Damascus-Jerusalem "shuttle" from May 29 to August 29, 1974, resulting in the Golan Disengagement Agreement, and President Hafez Asad's meetings with Carter and Vance in 1977, there had been no direct and little indirect official dialogue between Israel and Syria since the 1973 war. And unlike with Jordan (or with the Palestinians), there had been very few informal, secret contacts between Syria and Israel over the years. This absence of contact reflected Syria's rigid refusal to acknowledge Israel's legitimate existence as well as the isolation of President Asad's regime. Syrian political and popular attitudes were equally adamant in their rejection of Israel, and were marked by strong negative emotions and badly distorted stereotypes. Although Israel accepted Syria's legitimate existence and interest in seeking an agreement that would lead to Israeli withdrawal, Israeli attitudes toward Syria were also quite negative, reflecting a deep suspicion of the Asad regime and its intentions.

Working against this background, Secretary of State James Baker required eight trips to the region during 1991 as well as other meetings with top Syrian and Israeli leaders to obtain their agreement to attend the Madrid Conference and engage in direct bilateral talks for the first time. No progress at all had been made in starting the process of closing substantive gaps. Thus, when direct talks were about to begin in late October 1991, the two parties were actually still in the prenegotiation phase. This meant that the focus of effort by the United States (and USSR) during the initial period of talks would necessarily be directed on trying to establish a mutually receptive attitude toward discussion of the areas of difference and dispute between them rather than on detailed negotiations on specific issues. What would be required of the United States, as co-chair and chief facilitator/mediator of the talks, would be techniques similar to those used between the end of the 1973 war and 1977 to bring Egypt and Israel to the point where serious direct or indirect diplomatic discussion of issues was possible between them (compare Stein and Lewis, 1991).

Objective and Rationale

The Institute conceived of a policy-relevant simulation exercise in August 1991, at the same time that the U.S. peace initiative was gathering momentum. The project was designed by former Ambassador Samuel W. Lewis, President of the United States Institute of Peace, and former Ambassador Robert B. Oakley, Project Director and Senior Coordinator of the Institute's Special

Middle East Program in Peacemaking and Conflict Resolution, with the assistance of Major General Indar Jit Rikhye (Ret.), Senior Consultant to the Institute on United Nations Affairs, and generous and valuable advice from Professor (emeritus) Lincoln P. Bloomfield, Massachusets Institute of Technology.

The exercise was designed to reproduce as realistically as possible the dynamics of actual Syrian and Israeli representatives meeting face-to-face for the first time following a plenary session of the Middle East Peace Conference in Madrid. And, on four consecutive days (November 3-6, 1991), a policy-relevant simulation was conducted involving thirty-one people, seven of whom were support staff. Ambassador Oakley set out the following two-paragraph rationale in an exercise overview paper.[21]

> Following the 1973 war, Syrian military officials met Israelis under UN auspices to settle military issues, but claimed officially to be part of the Egyptian delegation. In the case of the March 1974 Golan disengagement agreement, Secretary of State Kissinger negotiated indirectly a formal, detailed agreement between the two which was endorsed and observed by the UN. This agreement has been carefully respected ever since its conclusion, by both parties. On other occasions, informal understandings were reached on the disposition of Syrian forces and weapons systems in the Lebanon-Israeli and Syrian-Lebanon border areas, notably the 1976 "Red Line" agreements. These understandings were never explicitly accepted but were nevertheless respected by Syria as well as by Israel. However, there have been no previous instances of direct, officially-blessed and acknowledged talks between Israeli and Syrian officials.

> Given the numerous and serious substantive and attitudinal differences between the two governments, there is great uncertainty as to the amount and nature of dialogue between them which would take place during a formal bilateral meeting, or in direct informal exchanges, and the effect of anticipated actions by the U.S. and the USSR in trying to facilitate direct or indirect dialogue and resolve differences between the Israelis and Syrians. These real-life uncertainties need to be explored thoroughly during the exercise, with the initiative coming primarily from the dynamism created by

the Syrian and Israeli teams in simulating accurately positions and negotiating tactics of their governments, and by the U.S. team in assisting/encouraging the process. Inputs will be made by control, as necessary, on procedural issues as well as on how the positions of the parties on various substantive issues affect their readiness for either a direct or indirect dialogue, how forthcoming the parties might be in substantive dialogue on specific issues, what roles are envisaged for the U.S., USSR and/or the UN [and other actors], and what outside events might be incorporated into the process.

Clearly, many objectives paralleled one or more of Cunningham's four distinct approaches while not precisely following any one approach. While we were interested in exploring decision-making processes, we were not attempting to generate new or to test existing theory—the *experimental approach* was discounted. Naturally, we were interested in achieving a better understanding of what might occur in the future, but, unlike the *predictive approach*, we were not constructing a formal model[22] for the explicit purpose of prediction or forecasting; there were no "payoff matrixes," and no attempts were made to ascertain probability. Furthermore, our interests were as focused on *why* something happened as they were on *what may* happen. This begins to merge with our interest in *evaluative approaches* in so far as we desired to assess how effective or ineffective modes of communication, a particular strategy, or a specific confidence-building measure might be. In regard to the *educational approach*, our primary objective was to generate sufficient new insight that a beneficial transfer of knowledge could occur between the respective players and their governments, thus assisting actual negotiations. We also hoped to learn something useful about the applicability of simulations for conflict resolution.

The Institute's policy exercise was therefore a structured yet flexible vehicle for confronting people with a model different from that with which they are comfortable; a great deal of useful insight can be gained from forcing people to challenge old assumptions and behavioral patterns, to broaden their perspective on the problems at hand, to think critically, and to problem-solve.[23] Consequently, the simulation was specifically designed and managed to be more process-oriented than to generate specific answers or solutions based on observed outcomes. This does not imply, however, that the exercise did not produce interesting and useful outcome-oriented insight—in fact, quite the opposite occurred.

Participant Selection

This process was guided by two basic principles: expertise and availability. Although it was conducted with full knowledge of the four real governments, the simulation was not an official exercise, and no current officials were asked to participate. However, two of our initially chosen players were subsequently asked by their governments to take part as advisors at the Madrid Conference. While this was a disappointment, it confirmed that we were targeting the best available experts. In regard to expertise, Lincoln Bloomfield suggests that "how successfully a simulation emulates reality depends on the extent of the players' knowledge of the structures, routines and probable responses of decisionmakers" (1984:785).

This criterion was especially crucial for our exercise because the players were required to simulate not only Syrian and Israeli diplomatic behavior but also to identify probable positions, responses, and likely decisions of the Asad and Shamir administrations as well as those of the United States and USSR. Most of the scholars had firsthand policy-relevant experience, while the former policymakers were quite senior and thoroughly grounded in the think-tank approach to conflict resolution. Whenever possible, Israeli, Soviet, and Syrian nationals with these backgrounds were chosen to reflect more accurately national thought processes and cultural predispositions.[24] In the end, eleven foreign nationals and thirteen Americans agreed to participate; of seven additional participants who assumed support roles, five were American[25] and two were foreign nationals.

There were four national teams (Syrian, Israeli, U.S., and USSR, with the latter two as co-chairs) and a Control team that monitored progress and provided external input when needed. Each team was composed of four to five individuals (three for the USSR and seven for Control), including a designated team leader, with considerable in-depth knowledge of the overall background—and especially of the policies, positions, strategies, and negotiating tactics and probable interaction tendencies of the governments they were supposed to be representing. Also included on each team was a rapporteur-liaison officer to assist the members in maintaining accurate accounts of their activities, to run messages, and to help keep Control updated. This allowed the exercise to unfold in as flexible and realistic a manner as possible, with minimum externally directed input from the Control team, which could have made for an artificial scenario and outcome.

Planning and Briefing

Several formal planning sessions were conducted at the Institute prior to the exercise, as were numerous informal sessions held among members of the Institute staff. Contrary to Toth (1988b), we avoided extensive preparatory meetings involving all the participants in order to preserve the realism and possibility of unprogrammed dynamic interaction that had been painstakingly built in. For example, prior to Madrid and the ensuing negotiations, many actual participants were strangers. While they might have known of one another and some may actually have met, most Syrians and Israelis have not engaged in direct, face-to-face talks.

Briefing books were provided to the participants as they boarded the bus. The transportation time between Washington, D.C., and the location where the simulation was held was then used as yet another planning session. Those participants who traveled on their own received the books in advance. Included in the briefing books was an overview paper with a checklist of substantive issues, the agenda, participants and team assignments, two background papers prepared by Institute staff ("1974 Syrian-Israeli Disengagement Agreement," "Lebanon: From the Red Lines to the Taif Accord"), reference material on basic documents and agreements, interviews and speeches from Madrid, biographies of Madrid participants, and a series of maps.

On the first evening there was a full plenary session designed to introduce the participants to one another and to the exercise. The methodology was presented along with the opening scenario and general procedural explanations, one of which is particularly noteworthy. The participants were informed of our belief that maximum realism would be obtained by each team playing its role "close to the vest," taking positions and reacting to external developments as would real-world delegations. Drawing on their knowledge of past and present governmental policies, positions, and attitudes, the teams were instructed to probe for possible openings in the heretofore blocked Syrian-Israeli dialogue. However, as no major agreements or breakthroughs on substantial issues could realistically be expected in the real world during the initial negotiating rounds, the teams were informed that they should not feel compelled to structure their play in order to achieve such ends. Rather, they should focus on communication-enhancing and confidence-building measures. In addition to formal meetings, all teams, but especially Israel and Syria, were urged to seek informal, private contexts in order to enhance communication.

The roles of the United States and the USSR during the simulation were also to parallel the real-world diplomacy of Secretary Baker. Following the agreement he worked out for the peace talks, the simulated U.S. and Soviet teams would be available to assist the participants if so requested, but they would not attempt to impose their views or take over the talks.

As to procedure, participants were told that the exercise was to have minimal structure in order not to retard the emergence of real-world dynamics, including the minimization of Control's *deus ex machina* role. Whereas the actual exercise was for three evenings and days, simulated time was to be much longer. Move periods were not predetermined, but were worked out in consultation between the teams and Control so as to allow the simulation of possible stages of Syrian-Israeli discussions, for example, initial explorations, probing for limited initiatives, and detailed discussions of possible limited agreement, once they emerged as sufficiently ripe for discussion. In the real world, several separate meetings would probably be needed for each of these stages and would involve formal discussion with accompanying informal communication (e.g., private meetings between heads of delegations, secret talks). However, the Institute simulation compressed this series of meetings into two days.

The majority of input from Control occurred via the exchange of messages between teams or between a team and its head of government. For example, participants were told that there were provisions for the teams to simulate communications to and receive instructions from capitals, with occasional input from Control, some of whose members assumed the role of chief of state or head of government for each respective negotiating team. The national teams were to portray the role of senior officials named by their respective governments as representatives to the Peace Conference. They were "instructed" by their governments with an initial position agreed in consultation between the members of each team and Control. As the exercise developed, team members—via the team leader and liaison—would receive from Control further government positions on important issues that arose, often in response to the teams' own recommendations or requests that evolved from the interplay with other teams.

Following the plenary, teams caucused separately for the remainder of the evening to discuss opening and fallback positions as well as longer-range strategy. Interactive play began early the next morning, when the initial scenario called for participants to start the second round of direct talks.

Beginning Play: Phase One

Control provided a guidance memorandum to set the stage for the second-round talks that summarized a hypothetical first round in which Israel and Syria had done virtually nothing more than reiterate, this time directly to one another, their previously stated positions. Israel had stated its position of peace (not territory) for peace; cited Syria's past record of aggression, their refusal to envisage true peace, and general lack of goodwill; and detailed present Syrian activities they viewed negatively (e.g., support for various forms of anti-Israeli and international terrorism, occupation of Lebanon, human rights violations and oppression of Syrian Jews, pressure upon other Arabs not to sit down with Israel, and major acquisitions of new weapons). Syria's first-round statements had focused on unlawful Israeli occupation of Arab land, insisted on the full implementation of United Nations Security Council Resolution (UNSCR) 242, and demanded the return of the Golan Heights, which had been illegally annexed by Israel. It mentioned the desirability of peace, but in the abstract rather than in terms of a Syrian-Israeli peace treaty with normal diplomatic relations, trade, and travel; in Syria's view, Israeli return of occupied territory would bring peace.

On Sunday night, November 3, in light of the basic situation postulated by Control, the Israeli team met to discuss its agenda for bilateral talks on Monday. The following were their main concerns:

- defining Israel's ultimate objective;
- defining Syria's ultimate objective;
- ascertaining the extent of U.S. pressure on Israel;

- reversing the decline of confidence in the United States as an "honest broker"; and
- gauging the increasing irrelevance of the Soviet Union.

The delegation outlined a basic strategy for the talks:

- Israel would offer peace for peace.
- The meaning of peace for Israel would be put forth.
- The meaning of peace for Syria would be pursued.
- The notion of "land for peace" would not be raised.

Should the Syrians push the issue of territory, Israel would turn to the United States, suggesting that concessions on two separate matters at once (i.e., vis-à-vis the Palestinians and the Syrians) were not possible and that there would be more hope of progress on the Palestinian-Jordanian negotiating front. Should Syria reject this argument, Israel would cable Jerusalem and inquire about the possibility of raising the issue of territorial concessions. The delegation concluded that the nature of the negotiations would change drastically if Asad were directly to convey his commitment to real peace to the Israeli people.

The Syrian delegation met Sunday night and strongly agreed that "land for peace" and UNSCR 242 were the only bases for discussion with Israel. It was also agreed that U.S.-Soviet active participation in the process was essential to any useful outcome. A basic ingredient of the Syrian strategy was time; the Syrians felt no great sense of urgency to conclude an agreement. Negotiations, it was agreed, could go on for an extended period, but the delegation did recognize the risk of the Palestinian-Israeli talks moving far enough ahead to outflank Syrian-Israeli talks.

Keeping President Bush satisfied was another central consideration for the Syrians. Concurrently, it seemed important to drive a wedge between the United States and Israel. The delegates agreed that Syria should increase its attention to public relations and speak directly to the Israeli and American publics. Syria would stress the importance of differentiating between the Likud government and the State of Israel (and its people). The bottom line was that Syria wanted the peace process to continue for as long as possible, but in no way did it want or could it afford to be seen as the cause of a breakdown. Clearly, Syria felt no urgency for a Syrian-Israeli agreement.

Prior to the opening of the bilateral talks, the Syrian delegation requested the presence of the U.S. and Soviet cosponsors at the Monday morning meeting. Citing the terms of the U.S.-Soviet invitation to Madrid, Israel denied the request for two reasons: because of concern about U.S. pressure, which was coupled with the feeling that the United States was not entirely an honest broker since it had chosen also to be to some degree a protagonist; and because the essential purpose of the talks was to give the two parties the chance to get to know each other and engage in a direct, clear exchange of positions, especially with regard to security fears. Israel wanted to hear a Syrian analysis as much as present its own. The United States and the Soviet Union, citing the terms of reference for Madrid, declined to attend.

Israel, in opening the bilateral session on November 4, referred to history, noting that it could not be ignored since it informs the present, stressed repeated Arab attacks upon Israel and rejection of its existence, and proffered a possible parallel for Syria with Israeli-Egyptian peace negotiations. Israel stressed its commitment to peace, reiterated its fundamental position that the recognition of Israel was absolutely necessary, and posed the question: How does Syria envision peace with Israel?

Syria downplayed the relevance of history to the present discussion, immediately raised the issue of UNSCR 242 and Israeli-occupied territory, and stated Syria's commitment to peace, noting that "what peace looks like" is less important than the most fundamental issues of withdrawal from territories and the restoration of Palestinian rights. Syria expressed the need for a "comprehensive peace," or peace that included all the parties in the region and resolved all issues of contention (especially the Israeli-Palestinian relationship). Syria reiterated its conviction that the content of peace could not be discussed until the territorial parameters within which such a peace would take place were defined.

The session ended with discussion, at Israel's initiative, of the idea of three "tracks" for the talks—peace, security, and territory. Both sides perceived these elements as necessary to the ensuing negotiations, although each held differing views as to the order, the relationship between, and the exact definition of these three elements. Israel wanted the primary focus on the first two, arguing that the issue of territory would therein be clarified and resolved. Syria wanted to focus first on territory and withdrawal. In the end it did not accept the Israeli separate track idea.

In informal talks following the first session, the Israelis felt that they had made a concession, but the Syrians either ignored it or failed to perceive it. At the urging of the U.S. and Soviet co-chairs, the Israelis decided to keep pursuing the issue. Their intention was to offer the Syrians a two-track approach: one working group would flesh out the nature of peace, while the second would focus on investigating security issues, including possible consideration of the notion of territorial adjustment.

The Israelis felt that more progress could be made if the head of their delegation met with the Syrian head. The offer was made and accepted. The Syrian head of delegation, after hearing the Israeli proposal, noted that territory was still being considered as a subsidiary issue, rather than the key initiating point. Syria could not back away from its basic notion that any permanent structure needed to be tied to a firm foundation: the principle of resolving the territorial issue in accordance with international law, namely UNSCR 242 (i.e., withdrawal).

At the meeting with the conference co-chairs on Monday afternoon, the Syrians expressed their dissatisfaction with the talks, saying that the "bilateral format is not working" and expressing their belief that the conference sponsors would have to step in to move the process forward. Syria told the co-chairs they were extremely disappointed that Israel would still not commit to "withdrawal" from Golan and stressed Damascus's view that territorial decisions could be made on the basis of security, which Israel says it wants. The Syrian delegation also suggested that Israeli comparisons to the peace process with Egypt were unrealistic, and that only breakthroughs on territorial concessions and overall positive Israeli behavior could bring about the "full peace" that Israel wants with Syria. Damascus was ready to discuss a "full" relationship with Israel, but only after an Israeli commitment to return all the Golan. Syria expressed a readiness to negotiate and conclude an agreement on the Golan that could include a demilitarized zone, if actual implementation were linked to a final agreement between the Israelis and the Palestinians. Absent any indications of Israeli flexibility or commitment on withdrawal, the Syrian delegation saw no point in continuing the talks.

U.S. and Soviet discussions with Israel and Syria after the bilateral meeting sought to clarify the Israeli proposal on separate tracks as a means of bridging the large gap. The Israelis expressed great skepticism about Syria's desire for peace, but said they would be prepared to talk about any issues, including territory (subject to authorization from their government), provided peace and security were also discussed. For its part, the Syrian team said it had not discerned at the formal session an Israeli readiness to discuss territory. They also said that Syria was unwilling to undertake any confidence-building measures (CBMs) except for the extension of Lebanese (and Syrian) control farther south in Lebanon. They made some specific proposals in this regard.

At this point a putative message from President Asad to Presidents Bush and Gorbachev was received by the U.S. and Soviet teams. South Lebanon and Israeli-Lebanese talks should take precedence over the Golan Heights in the negotiations, although Syria's intention to continue talking with Israel was reiterated. The U.S. team, though suspicious of Asad's real intentions (which they thought centered on freezing the Israeli-Palestinian talks without Syrian withdrawal from the overall process), told the Israeli team that the proposal might have some merit provided that other bilateral talks were not suspended. At this point, Control issued a situation update reporting several attacks on Israeli positions by terrorists operating out of Lebanon, including an attack on an outpost in the Golan Heights, very near Lebanon. News of the terrorist attacks on Israel halted any further discussion of the Asad suggestion. The Israelis were furious, convinced that Syria had inspired or facilitated these attacks as a means of pressuring Israel to change its position in the talks. Despite Syrian denials and a solemn message from President Bush to the Israeli government urging restraint, talks were temporarily suspended.

At a meeting with the Syrian delegation, the U.S. team, expecting Israeli retaliation for the terrorist attacks, told the Syrians that the United States hoped that once this "cycle of violence" was over the negotiations would continue. The U.S team also urged the Syrians to take stronger action against terrorists operating from Syria and to break completely from Hizb'allah. A message from President Bush to Asad reinforced these points. The Syrian delegation suggested that Syria might undertake some moves towards nonbelligerency if Israel would consider withdrawing from Golan or at least restoring Syrian sovereignty there. The Soviets then received a message from Asad condemning the terrorist attacks and announcing, as a sign of good faith, that he had closed the headquarters of Ahmad Jibril, whose organization was believed responsible for the attacks. Asad urged a three-month suspension of talks.

A U.S.-Soviet meeting was arranged with the Syrian and Israeli heads just before the Israeli delegation head returned to Jerusalem to confer about an appropriate response. The Syrian head pointed out that the Syrian delegation didn't walk out when Israel bombed south Lebanon, violated Syrian airspace, and launched new settlements. Why is the Israeli delegate walking out now? The Syrians, having turned to the Soviets for some support, were told "our government is preoccupied right now." The Soviet head also remarked that both sides needed to compromise.

Continuation of Play: Phase Two

At this point, Control, in consultation with the teams, decided that the initial and exploratory stages of the talks had been adequately and realistically played out. This would have taken a number of meetings over several weeks in actual negotiations (roughly the months of November-December). Although some glimmers of openings had been seen, serious, substantive dialogue was totally blocked by intransigence and suspicion on both sides. It would be necessary to allow simulated time to move ahead so that simulated but realistic external events could have an impact on the negotiations. Based on a realistic assessment of Israeli and Syrian policy, Control decided that talks should be resumed rather than suspended. Consequently, Control moved the simulated time ahead from December 1991 to February 1, 1992, and issued a new guidance memorandum. The key features of this new guidance memorandum are given below.

Palestine/Jordan/Israel talks have continued, vacillating between tense and relatively businesslike, but on the whole, progress has been satisfactory. Agreement in principle has been reached on a number of functions to be turned over to the Palestinians and on elections in the territories (with the question of East Jerusalem participation to be decided later). The U.S. and Soviet mediators have stayed in the background, but U.S. suggestions have helped achieve several compromises.

Multilateral talks have been held for three rounds with participants from all Arab governments except Syria and Lebanon; subcommittees for arms control, water, refugees, and economic development have been established. However, the Arabs have refused to get into any serious discussion of substantive issues until Israel indicates some acceptance of land for peace.

Syrian-Israeli talks have shown no progress, except that considerable informal dialogue between the parties has been occurring. The atmosphere has been improved by some corridor conversations about Lebanon on the fringes of Israeli-Syrian talks and by Israeli reference to "territorial adjustments." The United States had floated informally an idea for an interim move on the Golan, and neither government rejected it outright. The United States and the USSR would be allowed to be present as observers in upcoming bilateral talks.

Lebanese-Israeli talks have made some limited progress in discussing substantive issues, including phased reduction of Israeli Defense Forces (IDF) in south Lebanon, phased moves south by the Lebanese Armed Forces (LAF), LAF's assumption of control over areas from which the South Lebanese Army (SLA) withdraws, and disarmament of Hizb'allah. However, no agreements can be reached and no action taken until there is Syrian-Israeli movement.

Israel is in the midst of a political crisis and the early stages of a political campaign. The smaller parties have left the Shamir Government, which is now in a caretaker status. Elections have been set for mid-June; Levy, Sharon, and Arens are challenging Shamir for the Likud leadership. The major political issues are whether or not to move ahead with massive settlement activity, including the Golan; whether or not to agree to start implementing autonomy activities with Palestinians; how to improve absorption of Russian immigrants; and how to maintain satisfactory relations with the United States without yielding to Bush's "diktat." Settlements activity has been, in fact, minimal in recent months, which Shamir attributes to a shortage of funds. This trend is criticized vehemently by Sharon. Shamir's quiet assurances to Bush that he is holding the pace of settlements activity to a minimum have been relayed by Bush to Syria.

On another front, Hamas and certain Palestinian fringe groups have been stepping up demonstrations in the territories and terrorist activity against moderate Palestinians, although the Palestinian Liberation Organization (PLO)/Fatah forces remain dominant in Palestinian politics. The prestige of West Bank/Gaza leaders has continued to increase. Despite the increased unrest, Israeli public opinion reflects more optimism with regard to the prospects for the peace process.

Syria (Asad) is unhappy over continued Israeli reluctance to accept "land for peace" and has expressed his unhappiness to the co-chairs at highest levels, alleging backsliding from what he had been told

by Secretary of State Baker before agreeing to enter the talks. He
is also angry at the Palestinians for moving ahead on negotiations
for an interim arrangement and at the other Arabs for holding
initial multilateral meetings. Syrian-affiliated groups have been
stepping up guerrilla activity against Israel and other Arabs, especially in south Lebanon. Asad seems to be hinting at interest in
seeing an Israeli response to ideas the United States might put
forward on a "Golan II" interim agreement.

The United States Congress and the Bush Administration have agreed
on a loan guarantee program for one year only, in the wake of
private assurances from Shamir that no new settlements would be
begun (although some expansion/thickening will likely occur).
Secretary Baker is helping to produce progress in Israel-Jordan/
Palestine talks, but at the same time the United States continues
to press Israel on halting settlements as well as on signaling
some flexibility on the Golan and land for peace. Relations
between President Bush and Prime Minister Shamir are correct,
but not warm. President Bush's popularity remains high, the
Democratic presidential campaign remains confused, and
American public interest in the Middle East negotiations has
almost totally subsided.

This scenario change, presented Tuesday morning, November 5, obliged the U.S. team to try and establish some basis for
discussion of practical proposals for the Golan Heights. Meeting
first informally with Israeli and then with Syrian delegates, the
United States swiftly fashioned a proposal that would have Israeli
forces withdraw a very few kilometers from one or a few small
areas of the Golan Heights in return for a number of political
concessions from Syria in the direction of nonbelligerency. The
Syrian team thought the amount of territory to be given up by the
Israelis was too small to justify so many CBMs by Syria, which
included the creation of a joint Syrian-Israeli military commission,
the thinning out of forces in the Golan region, allowing Syria's
Jews to leave the country, and a declaration of nonbelligerency.
The U.S. team sought to counter Syrian objections by noting that
even a small territorial adjustment would "unfreeze the question

of Golan." The Syrians responded that they might be prepared to accept a modified proposal if the United States and Soviets gave a firm guarantee that there would be further progress on territory within a year.

In informal, "corridor" talks between individual members of the Israeli and Syrian teams, signals were exchanged of much greater willingness by their respective governments to at least consider a major interim agreement on the Golan. The rigid insistence of each government that the other must show willingness to take the first step toward concessions, at least in principle, frustrated the delegates and stymied serious negotiations or even detailed discussions of the other government's vital concerns (e.g., peace for Israel, withdrawal for Syria). There was, however, agreement on the need for much more informal dialogue as an essential complement to the sterile formal talks. Informal dialogue, it was felt, could bring the governments to drop their mirror-image insistence that the other party first accept their position, in principle at least. Means were discussed whereby that might occur. However, the conclusion was that neither Shamir's government, under present political circumstances, nor President Asad were prepared to push such talks.

In the formal bilateral meeting between Syria and Israel on Tuesday morning, to which the United States and the Soviet Union were invited initially as observers and then as full participants, the two sides took up a U.S. proposal. Since the Israeli-Syrian talks had not even found a way to begin discussing an overall peace treaty, the United States suggested that Syria and Israel aim instead to reach an interim agreement on a few key points. This would enable some common ground to be found, thereby keeping alive the momentum of Madrid and serving as yet another step toward a final settlement. The U.S. proposal, though focused narrowly on three areas, specified what should be included in any such interim agreement:

- A territorial component, that is, some kind of shift in boundaries—such as Israeli withdrawal from the town of

Majdal Shams—without which Syrians could not accept any agreement.

- A political component, modeled on Sinai II, that would transcend any military arrangement and that would include such CBMs as a joint renunciation of war and a commitment to eventual peace with open borders, economic relations, and other similar elements.
- Security arrangements, such as a thinning out of forces, a joint military commission, and shared responsibility for military control for south Lebanon.

The Syrians, though clearly interested, were wary of American assurances that an interim agreement would not prejudice terms of a final peace treaty. They quarreled with the very term "interim agreement," arguing that Syria could at best talk about a transitional agreement firmly rooted in the principle of "land for peace" that would be part and parcel of the process leading to a final treaty.

Nonetheless, under U.S. prodding and the Israelis' plea that the discussion not get bogged down in definitions, the Syrians asked for specific answers from the Israelis to four main questions. During an "interim" or "transitional" agreement, would the Israelis

— be ready, as a precondition for any agreement, to halt construction of settlements in the occupied territories;

— agree to a certain date for resuming the talks on a final treaty;

— allow Syrians displaced from the occupied Golan territories to return to their towns and villages and resume their lives; and

— begin withdrawal from southern Lebanon?

The Israelis answered with their own list of questions. Would Syria

— pledge not to obstruct ongoing negotiations between Israel and Jordan on the one hand and Israel and the Palestinians on the other;

— deliver a personal and public declaration in Arabic by President Asad to the Syrian people, rejecting war as a means of settling problems with Israel;

— allow several thousand Syrian Jews to emigrate to Israel;

— join the multilateral talks with other regional parties;

— agree to the formation of a mixed Syrian-Israeli military commission to deal with minor border problems and to the expansion of the United Nations Disengagement Observer Force (UNDOF) buffer zone to the east; and

— stop all anti-Israeli propaganda internationally and within Syria and end its support of terrorist organizations?

The Syrians, while explaining that they obviously could not answer those questions without consulting Damascus, did offer some hints as to what those answers might be. They reiterated Syria's determination not to interfere in Israel's parallel bilaterals with the Palestinians and Jordan, but warned that it would honor its bilateral agreements with the government of Lebanon to coordinate policies. They also played down the issue of Syrians Jews, saying that it was purely an internal matter and that Damascus was already taking steps to deal with those cases that had been brought to their attention. The Syrians then held out the possibility that certain military cooperation measures might be worked out "in the right context" and that Damascus would not consider this to be a fundamental problem.

The Israelis responded that they would accept a peace treaty with Syria similar in form to the one they have with Egypt. Moreover, they explicitly put the issue of settlements in the occupied territories on the table as part of the overall negotiations. But they dodged Syria's request to set a date for resumption of such negotiations, and they said the matter of what do do about Lebanon should be separated from other issues unless Syria was ready to raise the whole question of the presence of Syrian forces in Lebanon.

Stopping Play

After several exchanges that basically repeated and reiterated previous conditions and positions, the Syrians and Israelis realized that they had reached an end to the current discussion and were now beginning to move in circles. The Israeli chief of delegation moved to adjourn so that he could report back to Jerusalem and ask for further instructions. The Syrian delegation agreed.

At this point, Control reviewed the entire exercise both in terms of what had been achieved in pursuing the original objectives and in terms of the real-world policies and positions of the governments concerned. It concluded that there was little more to be gained from further exploration of limited measures and improving communication without a fundamental shift in policy by Israel on withdrawal or by Syria on peace, and that such policy shifts would violate the norm of realism on which the simulation was based. While play could have continued in an effort to develop a mechanism to break the impasse, Control felt that this would not be a good use of time for the majority of participants. Thus Control signaled all four teams that the simulation was to be terminated.

In order to maximize the benefits for the policymakers, Control and the team leaders decided to devote the remaining time Tuesday afternoon to a group discussion of the Middle East peace process in light of both the simulation and what had occurred in Madrid, where the plenary session had just concluded and the three bilateral meetings had begun.

Before adjournment, the chief American representative said that Washington and Moscow were pleased with the progress. Some useful ideas on an interim settlement had emerged and been discussed. Both the Israeli and Syrian delegations were showing interest in a package of these proposals, and although there was no commitment, the package had been sent to Jerusalem and Damascus for review. There was hope for some sort of agreement. However, he cautioned both sides that the U.S. and Soviet peoples were losing interest in and patience with the Middle East stale-mate. He warned Syria and Israel that they should not assume that they could continue to enjoy the same levels of support from the superpowers as in the past. The United States and the Soviet Union had new and overriding domestic constraints of their own and would likely show impatience with any further intransigence or foot-dragging on the part of either party.

3

Post-Mortem

Lessons Learned: Reviewing Middle East Peace Prospects

The simulation was sufficiently complex and the players sufficiently expert in both their simulated roles and in their real-life capacities to warrant two distinct debriefing sessions during the exercise. One focused on the simulation itself; the exercise was debriefed in terms of both substance and process. The other occurred out of role; the participants, as professional analysts, felt it worthwhile to discuss the actual diplomatic and negotiating situation in light of what insight and new knowledge they had gained as a result of participating in the simulation. Both discussions proved interesting and useful with regard to implications for the future evolution of the Middle East peace process as well as for advancing the fields of negotiation and conflict resolution.

This group of highly experienced, intelligent observers of the Middle East scene was upbeat for the near term, but was neither optimistic nor pessimistic for the longer-run future. There was unanimous agreement that a policy-oriented discussion of the peace process was useful and that it substantially benefited from the tight, realistic focus and tough give-and-take of the simulation. There was debate over the long-term implications of the plenary conference and bilateral meetings in Madrid. Had a new dynamic emerged that would provide enough momentum for major changes on the ground? How much of a U.S. role would be required to maintain any such momentum? The best judgment was that a new dynamic had been unleashed, and it was exemplified by

- a change in Israeli attitudes toward the Palestinian delegation, which Israel decided to meet with separately, without the Jordanian figleaf, and whose contacts with the PLO it decided to ignore;
- the decision of the Jordanians and Palestinians to proceed with their bilateral meetings and that of Arab governments to proceed with the first multilateral meetings despite Syrian reservations, with Saudi Arabia playing a very positive role;
- Syrian and Israeli participation, despite irritations and mutual loss of diplomatic struggles and the desire of both not to be the first one to walk out;
- the warm Israeli domestic response to Shamir's handling of the Madrid situation, including talks with Palestinians and the tough response to Syria, and also to Bush's speech, which calmed somewhat the resentment of perceived U.S. pressure and bias against Israel (e.g., loan guarantees, criticism of overflights); and
- the positive Palestinian and Arab reaction to both the role of the Palestinian delegation and the resultant respect and recognition it was given internationally, the sharp diminution in sympathy for "rejectionists," and the open admiration for the essential and causal role played by the United States.

The consensus was that sufficient momentum had been built to move ahead quite far on the Palestinian autonomy or transitional arrangements talks, although the United States would need to intervene when major issues arose and when the time came to decide whether to sign a partial agreement on transition or wait for progress on Israeli-Syrian and other talks. There was no consensus on whether Syria would ultimately try to block such a separate, interim agreement and, if that occurred, whether other Arab pressure would overcome such opposition.

The group also felt that neither Syria nor Israel presently sees strong incentives for a major new agreement between them, interim or permanent. The security risks are not that great, the political pressures on both sides against concessions are powerful, and the long history of suspicion weighs strongly on the process. Thus, major outside incentives and assistance will be required to achieve any large-scale agreement. Syria might be amenable to a small, ad hoc transitional arrangement, particularly if Israel and the Palestinians were about to conclude a separate interim agreement, but outside assistance as well as Israeli reciprocity would still be required. Israel is apparently not ready for another formal interim agreement with Syria unless any such agreement signifies much more of a commitment to peace than did the 1975 Sinai II agreement with Egypt, but Syria appears ready to accept only an interim or transitional agreement with less of a commitment to nonbelligerency than Sinai II. Therefore, de facto, parallel unilateral steps appear to offer the best opportunity of producing a limited additional move on the Golan. The group formulated two major suggestions for procedural methods to facilitate serious dialogue:

- urge Israel and Syria to use the "three-track" approach of parallel discussions on withdrawal, security, and peace; and
- urge Israel and Syria to talk on a hypothetical, reciprocal basis; that is, we could do this (spell it out) on peace or withdrawal if you could agree to withdrawal from Golan, guarantee of peace, and so forth.

Another insight relating to the Syrian-Israeli dynamic was the great Israeli sensitivity to the security of Galilee from attack originating in Lebanon. The Israeli assumption that Syria controls whatever activity takes place in Lebanon—regular or irregular, Palestinian, Lebanese, or Syrian—causes Israel to place great importance, in terms of Israeli-Syrian relations, on any challenge to the South Lebanese Army and the IDF units in the "security zone" in south Lebanon. The Israeli team's strong negative reaction to simulated attacks out of south Lebanon and a simulated Asad proposal to talk with Israel about Lebanon rather than continuing with bilateral issues was seen as an accurate reflection of this fundamental Israeli attitude.

This simulation reinforced participant convictions that a strong leadership role for the United States in such a negotiating process is crucial. However, opinions were mixed over how much time there would be for negotiations, whether or not the United States should force the pace, and how much influence the United States could actually have over the negotiating process. The overall judgments seemed to be that the United States ought to work on all issues, giving priority to concluding an Israeli-Palestinian interim agreement while probing readiness for a limited partial Israeli-Syrian agreement and helping lay the groundwork for a big push on the issues in 1993.

One participant warned against being overconfident in the ability of the parties, even with U.S. help, to sustain negotiations over a longer period of time. He pointed out that one assumption behind the Baker initiative is that the act of getting the parties together creates a dynamic of its own and that the longer they sit together, the more they'll recognize the need for peace. He warned that this assumption might be erroneous. It may very well be that the longer the two parties sit together, the clearer their differences will become and the more certain their repulsion for one another's positions. Therefore, from his point of view, it is dangerous to be complacent about the role of time.

The group agreed that one should not count for long on either the status quo or more favorable trends prevailing in the Middle East. The inherent volatility of the region, the presence of politico-religious fanatics, demagogues, and movements working to disrupt any progress toward compromise, and the vulnerabilities of all regional governments militate against complacency. Moreover, the growing Israeli distrust of tight U.S. political constraints on Israeli freedom of action comes at a time when the USSR is no longer a factor in the region and U.S. political and military support is less crucial for Israel's security.

The Israeli and U.S. participants were unanimous in recognizing the serious problem posed by the absence of parallel channels for informal communications (or secret talks) to advance Syrian-Israeli negotiations. The United States had helped Israel and Egypt establish a dialogue after the 1973 war, but communications via the United States were supplemented by a number of vitally important direct, authorized, confidential contacts. Israel was believed to be ready for and able to maintain the confidentiality of such contact. President Asad needs to make the decision to permit them if much negotiating progress is to occur. The sudden flowering of Palestinian support for negotiation owes a great deal to years of quiet dialogue among newer Palestinian leaders and Israelis as well as Americans, Europeans, and others, and their participation in private meetings with Israelis, other Arabs, and non-Arabs.

Concerning a related issue—the role of public diplomacy in reinforcing the negotiating process—there was unanimity that Asad should draw a lesson from Sadat's earlier efforts starting in 1974, and not focus merely on the Egyptian president's 1977 visit to Jerusalem, which Asad is unlikely to replicate. The government of Israel also needs to exercise greater constraint and assert greater control over actions (and actors) clearly destructive of the peace process (e.g., new settlement on the Golan and in other occupied territories, imposing tighter security restrictions on Palestinians). The government should also dissociate itself publicly from such actions.

Paralleling actual events, the simulation led almost all of the participants to the conviction that a leadership role for the United States in this kind of negotiation is crucial. Based on the experience of the simulation, participants concluded that the United States could assist in the formulation and promotion of overall cooperation and better relations in the following specific ways. First, the United States can establish the mechanism for cooperation so that disjointed efforts can be coordinated in some progression toward low-risk moves. (The Syrian team insisted on U.S. involvement for this reason.) Second, the United States can help with the identification of common goals. Third, the United States can assist in identifying a theory of cost/benefit distribution that otherwise seemed to be lacking.

The group disagreed sharply, however, on the nature and degree of intensity of U.S. involvement. As in all Middle East negotiations involving the United States over the past twenty-five years, the Arabs (in this case Syrians) demanded more direct, active U.S. involvement, not only in terms of making recommendations to the parties but even to the extent of imposing them on Israel. Israel, in turn, accepted the need for some U.S. involvement but insisted that it be essentially passive, procedural, and nonsubstantive.

Lessons Learned: Reviewing the Simulation Process

As observed earlier and described in the scenarios provided to the teams by Control, this particular policy exercise was restricted in design to what the Institute considered the most realistic degree of diplomatic dialogue achievable between Israel and Syria during an initial feeling-out phase that would take place prior to Israeli elections in mid-1992. For the time being, it was assumed that there was no chance of Israel's accepting the principle of total withdrawal and therefore no chance of Syria agreeing to talk about comprehensive peace. Nor was there any likelihood that the United States would attempt to force either or both of the parties to make major concessions. The simulation objective was thus to study the nuances of negotiation and prenegotiation in the initial bilateral encounters (the process of developing mutual familiarity) rather than to explore in detail or try to conclude substantive agreements, either interim or final. This

objective produced some critical comments, including some dis-
agreement by participants.

Both the Israeli and Syrian delegations agreed that the dynamic
that evolved during the simulation was quite realistic. The parties
clearly had difficulty with communication, and movement was
minimal. The simulated dynamic—slow and painful as it was—
accurately reflected the real world. Gradually some "glimmers"
had begun to emerge from this dynamic, but Control had delib-
erately refrained from pushing harder, although Control did
suggest that informal meetings be arranged. Based on the real-
world experience of the participants, they agreed that informal
dialogue has been crucial to the successful conclusion of most
agreements. Few, if any, informal contacts between the Israelis
and the Syrians took place during the game, in spite of Control's
encouragement. The lack of "corridor" or "couch" diplomacy,
participants believed, limited the results of the exercise.

The Israeli team claimed that the Syrian government did not
allow its delegates to speak informally with the Israelis. (One
possibility would have been for Control to override the Syrian
position. It chose not to do so.) Syrian team members admitted
their intention not to appear overeager and to avoid rushing to
make concessions, which resulted in a deliberate initial standoff-
ishness that may have conveyed a reluctance to meet informally.
Another player suggested that in the real world Syria is suspicious
of secret talks, specifically secret U.S.-Israeli deals at its expense,
and is therefore more reluctant to agree to "informal" discussions.
Yet another explanation was that there simply was not enough
time to develop informal talks. The players felt they had too much
work to do in the time available. In addition, the players did not
simulate their roles outside of the meeting room as much as
Control had requested and hoped.

An Israeli suggested that the real-world Syrians could learn
from the Syrian role players. During the simulated negotiations, the Syrian team, when pushed, made concessions, spoke of
eventual full peace, and showed signs of permitting changes in

Israeli-Syrian relations. Although the Israelis saw clear discrepancies between the play-acted position and that of Asad's government, the lessons were evident nonetheless. The Syrian delegation responded that it did go further in the game than a real Syrian government might have gone, but was careful to do so more in form than substance. The idea was that anything the Syrians had agreed to or said in the past was not "off limits" or irrevocable. In this sense, by discussing security arrangements and talking about "comprehensive peace," they were not breaking ground. Where they did break ground, from the Syrian team's point of view, was in their suggestion that certain elements of negotiation would not be excluded if some assurances could be conceded or not excluded by the Israelis on other elements. In this way, without committing, the team opened the way for discussion.

Several participants thought that the U.S. role had been played too diffidently. One commentator suggested that in the real world, the United States would intervene in ways that were uncomfortable to the parties and would force them to act, as it was doing in Madrid. The overly passive role of the United States was perceived as a symptom of a structural problem with the simulation—a lack of outside pressures. For example, he believed that the Israeli-Syrian exchanges did not reflect the type of outside pressures that both sides would be exposed to in a real situation. This was clear in both the U.S.-Israeli relationship as well as Syria's relationship to other Arab states, particularly Saudi Arabia and Egypt. Such pressures would make for a more complicated game, but from this point of view, they would have resulted in more progress between the Israelis and Syrians.

Several participants also noted the need to induce confidence-building measures more successfully. During the simulation, the quest to sweeten the negotiation atmosphere by means of CBMs did not get very far. From one participant's point of view, this was due partly to the way in which the CBMs were proposed. Each side was asked to concede something in an unreciprocated way, and neither side was willing to initiate a concession.[26] Because

CBMs typically take place through informal channels, Control should put more thought into how to provide incentives outside of or in conjunction with the direct exchange between the two parties (e.g., offers of economic support by wealthy Arab states, the European Community, and Japan to Syria; offers of assistance to or implication of pressure on Israel).

According to one of the participants, the simulation would have profited if the Americans and Soviets had taken part as participants, rather than observers. The U.S. and Soviet teams benefited very little from the first bilateral discussion because they were not present. It would have been useful for them to have been there, he added, "in order to get a sense of how they were starting to set sparks off one another." (Control considered such an arrangement and decided against a more active U.S. role because it would go beyond anticipated U.S. behavior in the actual negotiations. U.S. and/or Soviet participation in the formal meetings had been made contingent upon approval by both parties under the Madrid Agreement.)

There was a feeling among several participants that Control not only should have applied more pressure on the negotiating process (including inducing CBMs) and on the U.S. team to play a more interventionist role but also should have floated hypothetical scenarios involving substantive issues and possible solutions, so that team leaders could at least gauge the reaction of their teams. Finally, Control should have had better knowledge of what each of the teams was thinking and planning as well as of all messages exchanged between teams.

Admittedly, both participants and students of Middle East negotiations would have found it more stimulating to negotiate or hypothesize solutions or agreements on substantive issues. This is often standard simulation fare. However, in this case, the more limited freedom of action corresponded to the specific purpose for which the exercise was conducted.

The authors conclude that the simulation was properly organized to achieve its objective in terms of minimizing artificial external pressures and the degree of envisioned U.S. activism and not moving to the stage of floating hypothetical scenarios regarding one or more specified substantive issues that might then lead to simulated interim or final agreements. In retrospect, Control could have done more to provide the parties with possible CBMs, particularly those involving parties not represented in the simulation (e.g., Japan, other Arab states, the EC, the UN). Real-world developments in the Madrid talks and subsequent negotiations in the Israeli-Syrian working group during the eight months since the simulation exercise have closely parallelled the actual conduct as well as the planned purpose of the simulation. One major objective of the exercise and subsequent report was to provide the opportunity for participants, observers, and government representatives to plan for what realistically lay ahead, including obstacles to movement on substantive issues. And judging from press reports, the Israeli and Syrian "slight flexibility" and contingent "what if" approach to substantive issues during the simulation has been the approach taken by both in practice. This sort of tentative exploration of views, even when positions differ sharply, gradually evolved between Egyptians and Israelis after 1973 and seems to be beginning to occur between Syrians and Israelis. Similarly, cautious unilateral substantive signals (not concrete, official proposals) seem to be emerging as a result of this present dialogue, as they did during the warming of Egyptian/Israeli relations. In this regard, the simulation was successful in stimulating both potential ideas and mechanisms and channels for a negotiating process that will inevitably be slow to unfold.

Criticism of Control for not being informed fully or for not providing for more discussion of ideas that emerged after the initial round of negotiations in the limited time available is valid. By being better informed, Control could have moved the simulated negotiation process along more rapidly, particularly during the second round. Part of the problem might have been alleviated by the use of a closed circuit television system and/or better organized systems of liaison. "Detrimental time lags" in reporting and communication were also a problem. This was, in some part, due to inadequate physical arrangements. Team rooms should be arranged to ensure privacy but at the same time be located in one central area so that participants have easy access to one another as well as to Control, whose base, incidentally, should be close to the team rooms but far enough away so that some sense of autonomy can be maintained.

It was suggested that it would be useful to include social psychologists or communication experts as part of Control, as separate observers, or as liaisons for Control. In this manner, they could help Control to be more fully informed and to understand better the dynamics of the exercise as it is played out. This suggestion was derived from a comment during a debriefing that the more traditional meaning of the term "security" should be broadened to include social-psychological elements. Attitudes, perceptions, values, needs, and fears are as real as economic conditions, geopolitical considerations, and military capabilities, especially as they impact on and are influenced by one another. These experts would be asked to observe and reflect on the role or impact of the human dimension on both the simulation and the reality that it models.

The relationship between the objective of the exercise and the individuals chosen to participate is extremely important. For example, if the main objective is to attempt to *understand better the likely real-world dynamics*, then process is equally important, if not more important, than outcome. Consequently, great care must be taken to secure participants who, while not official, are knowledgeable and representative of the positions and views of their respective governments. For this simulation, we were fortunate to have had such individuals. On the other hand, if the main objective is *actively to seek solutions to the various problems*, it becomes necessary to include people who are able to think critically and creatively, who can move beyond the "party line" and act as conceptual catalysts. Under this scenario, Control would have to be ready to assume a more interventionist role, since it would likely be responsible for proposing or even pushing alternative approaches.

Not to be overlooked is the distinction between designing and conducting simulations that are primarily policy planning tools and those that are specific participant training exercises. Depending on the amount of time available and the extent to which the designers hope to gain significant insights into possible outcomes, an attempt to integrate both objectives into one exercise might well yield much less than desired. Dividing the simulation into two specific segments or having two separate simulations would be more useful. After a thorough review of the "real-world dynamics" exercise, we believe that constructing a second simulation designed to explore possible creative solutions to the same problems and issues addressed during the first simulation should prove more practical.

In Conclusion

A policy exercise is one tool that can concurrently provide an opportunity to test various conflict resolution strategies, to examine the possible consequences of particular decisions and the impact of deliberate or unintentional external events, and to explore ways to improve communication among conflicting parties. In this regard, the participation of individuals in a simulation with full knowledge of their respective governments, or even involving official representatives in a nonbinding, unofficial exercise, may be a powerful complement to the prenegotiation process.[27] It furnishes an excellent medium in which the theory-practice nexus can generate policy-relevant information that would be difficult to acquire by any other means. As Brewer suggests, "A fundamental purpose of manual gaming is to encourage creative, innovative thinking about problems that defy treatment with more conventional approaches and methods" (1984:811). In short, a policy exercise can be a powerful implement in the peacemaker's tool kit.

In the end, this policy simulation exercise and events during the actual negotiations offered added evidence that general rules and theories of negotiation and conflict resolution behavior do apply to the Arab-Israeli conflict, provided they are properly and realistically applied. Moreover, this exercise demonstrated clearly that the use of simulations can be a rich method for studying the dynamics of conflict and conflict management. These results suggest that carefully designed simulation exercises should perhaps become a more routine part of attempts both to prevent and to resolve international conflict.

Notes

1. Bracken also notes that gaming and game theory can easily be confused, especially because of their similar names. Opposed to games, "game theory is a body of primarily mathematical theory concerning decisionmaking" (792).

2. See Becker (1980) for an additional view on the history of simulation and gaming.

3. For a good illustration of the evolution of chess and chesslike war games, see Wood (1972).

4. See also Brewer and Shubik (1979).

5. Paul Davis of the RAND Corporation has been working with a simulation based on a computer model that can be stopped to allow human decision-makers to play out a situation and feed new input into the computer. In essence, such a hybrid provides a mechanism for attempting to incorporate human proclivities.

6. It is interesting to note that Cunningham bases his argument on the premise that each of the four simulation approaches is being conducted by a *researcher* operating on the basis of formal social scientific goals and objectives. It is important to note, however, that the Institute simulation was not, in a traditional social science sense, testing specific research questions.

7. IIASA's forte, as a research organization, is experimental and descriptive modeling with prescriptive elements. They, perhaps more than any of the other organizations, run the gamut on method and purpose. Their organizational foci go far beyond international negotiation, and they are equally if not more concerned with process than with outcome.

8. ICS also offers a wide array of non-foreign policy exercises, including global geography, environmental decision-making, U.S. history and government, Europe 2010, and several others.

9. See Carr (1946) and Morgenthau (1973).

10. A third debate has emerged in the mid-1980s and continues to actively engage scholars in the question, "Whither international relations theory?" For a good review, see Yosef Lapid (1989), "The third debate: On the prospects of international theory in a post-positivist era," *International Studies Quarterly*, 33 (3): 235-254. There are several other solid articles in the same volume. Moreover, a special edition of *International Studies Quarterly* was devoted to this and similar issues. See Richard Ashley and R. B. J. Walker, eds. (1990), ISQ 34 (3).

11. For well-developed structural or systemic perspectives, see Waltz (1959 and 1979) and Gilpin (1981). At the opposite pole, the following are among those who deeply acknowledge an individualistic approach to the referents of conflict and its resolution: Jervis (1976); Ronald Fisher (1990)—chapter 6 provides a detailed description of a laboratory simulation known as the Intergroup Conflict Simulation; and Druckman (1973 and 1977). For a thorough review of the causes of war, see Levy (1989).

12. In this regard, see Choucri (1991). For a good treatment on the complex nature of conflict, see Mitchell (1981).

13. For insight into the influence of culture upon negotiations and diplomatic relations, see Cohen (1990 and 1991). See also Anand (1981) and Glen Fisher (1982 and 1988).

14. Harold Saunders has produced a very insightful treament on the need to improve communication between nations, and the need to develop an ability to think critically and to reframe situations/ problems in a more cooperative light. See "Beyond US and THEM—Building Mature International Relationships: The Role of Official and Supplemental Diplomacy." Unpublished manuscript, Brookings Institution, Washington, D.C. See also Saunders (1990).

15. For a comprehensive treatment of various dimensions of communication, see Korzenny and Ting-Toomey (1990).

16. This is a major premise underlying the problem-solving workshop approach of Herbert Kelman, John Burton, and Jay Rothman. It is also consistent with Ronald Fisher's concept of consultative third-party intervention.

17. See Dennis Sandole, "Simulation as a basis for consciousness raising: Some encouraging signs for conflict resolution," in David Crookall and Danny Saunders, eds. (1989), *Communication and Simulation: From Two Fields to One Theme* (Clevedon, England: Multilingual Matters). This volume provides a comprehensive treatment on the utility of simulation that not only spans the theory/practice divide, but extends across a number of applied contexts.

18. To the knowledge of the authors, there are not many instances where prominent diplomats specifically discussed their use of academic theory. For example, former Assistant Secretary of State Chester Crocker once commented that many of Herbert Kelman's theoretical insights were useful during his Namibia and Angola experiences. The theory/practice nexus is the subject of a forthcoming book by Alexander George (1993). In July 1992, the Institute also sponsored a major conference, "Dialogues on Conflict Resolution: Bridging Theory and Practice," which examined this issue in regard to five major conflicts (Kashmir, Peru, Mozambique, Yugoslavia, and Nagorno-Karabakh), and four thematic panel discussions ("Bridging Research and Practice," "Present Trends and Needs in the World Market for Conflict Resolution," "Domestic and International Based Approaches: How Can One Inform the Other?" and "The Causes and Dynamics of Conflict: What do Conflict Resolvers Need to Know?"). Publications based on the five conflict discussions and the four panels are forthcoming.

19. See also Brewer's chapter, "Discovery Is Not Prediction," in an excellent short book edited by Goldberg et al. (1990).

20. Simulation tools are frequently employed by police, the FBI, and many branches of the armed services. Flight simulators, "shoot-out" exercises, and others are quite common. It is also somewhat ironic that thousands of hours and millions of dollars are expended in order to select and train top athletes for international competition. Why should it be so strange to adapt technologies and techniques for training diplomats? After all, much more is at stake than a gold medal.

21. Internal unpublished document drafted September 17, 1991, and revised October 15, 1991, by Ambassador Robert Oakley, United States Institute of Peace, Washington, D.C.

22. In so far as the weaving of a complicated scenario can be considered a "summary of the variables occurring in reality" (Cunningham's definition of a model, p. 220), then all free-form simulations, ours included, are models.

23. Jay Rothman has argued the importance of critical thinking and in so doing turned to Stephan Brookfield's (1987) cogent articulation: "When we become critical thinkers we develop an awareness of the assumptions under which we, and others, think and act. We learn to pay attention to the context in which our actions and ideas are generated. We become skeptical of quick-fix solutions, of single answers to problems, and of claims to universal truth. We also become open to alternative ways of looking at, and behaving in, the world."

24. Bloomfield (personal communication with Lewis Rasmussen, April 29, 1992) distinguishes between a "realistic, representational strategy, or a normative strategy that is designed to evoke original or unorthodox ideas." Noting that both have merit depending on desired objectives, Bloomfield cautions against the representational strategy when using officials because they frequently are too constrained with "classified information, genuine contingency plans, etc." His extensive experience has led him frequently to adopt a role-reversal approach when designing or assigning roles. This approach frequently assists (or forces) the participant to think critically, to be more empathic, and to learn by developing greater understanding of multiple perspectives on a given issue, problem, or phenomenon. Having our participants undergo significant cognitive and behavioral change was not our primary intention. If this did occur, all the better. However, we tasked our participants to model a dynamic as closely as possible so that any insight we developed as to the likely patterns and outcomes of such actual interaction could be fed back to the policy communities of the respective countries. Furthermore, it was our belief that the former government officials who were participants had been absent from office for a sufficient time so as not to be constrained by an inability to disclose information. In fact, a former high-ranking Israeli military officer gave a very informative briefing on strategic considerations underlying Israeli withdrawal from the Golan that most participants found extremely current.

25. The label "American" is not intended to slight other culture groups who rightfully fall under this category, but rather refers to citizens of the United States of America.

26. Charles Osgood's GRIT (Graduated and Reciprocated Initiatives in Tension-Reduction) strategy, originally developed in the early 1960s, is predicated on at least one party being willing to offer some type of unilateral concession and continue to do so even if such overtures are not reciprocated. For a concise review of the strategy, see Osgood (1980).

27. As Zartman notes, "prenegotiation is a purposive period of transition that enables parties to move from conflicting perceptions and behaviors (unilateral attempts at solutions) to cooperative perceptions and behaviors" (1989:7). For insight into the theory and practice of prenegotiation, see Stein (1989). See also Saunders (1985), Laue et al. (1988), Laue (forthcoming), and a special edition of *The Jerusalem Journal of International Relations*, 13 (1991), edited by Jay Rothman.

References

Anand, R. P., ed. (1981). *Cultural Factors in International Relations*. New Delhi: Abinhav.

Becker, Henk A. (1980). "The emergence of simulation and gaming," *Simulation & Games*, 11 (1): 11-25.

Bercovitch, Jacob (1986). "International mediation: A study of the influence, strategies and conditions of successful outcomes," *Cooperation and Conflict*, 21: 155-167.

———— (1991). "International negotiations and conflict management: The importance of prenegotiation," *Jerusalem Journal of International Relations*, 13: 7-21.

Bloomfield, Lincoln P. (1992). Personal correspondence, April 29.

———— (1984). "Reflections on gaming," *Orbis*, 27 (4): 783-790.

Bracken, Paul (1984). "Deterrence, gaming, and game theory," *Orbis*, 27 (4): 790-802.

Brewer, Gary D. (1984). "Child of neglect: Crisis gaming for politics and war," *Orbis*, 27 (4): 803-812.

———— (1986). "Methods for synthesis: Policy exercises." In W. C. Clark and R. E. Munn, eds., *Sustainable Development of the Biosphere*. New York: Cambridge University Press. Pp. 455-473.

Brewer, Gary D., and Martin Shubik (1979). *The War Game: A Critique of Military Problem Solving*. Cambridge, Mass.: Harvard University Press.

Brookfield, Stephan (1987). *Developing Critical Thinkers: Challenging Adults to Explore Alternative Ways of Thinking and Acting*. San Francisco, Calif.: Josey-Bass Publishers.

Burton, John (1969). *Conflict and Communication: The Use of Controlled Communication in International Relations.* London: Macmillan.

Carr, E. H. (1946). *The Twenty Years' Crisis.* London: St. Martin's Press.

Choucri, Nazli (1991). "Analytical and behavioral perspectives: Causes of war and strategies for peace." In Thompson and Jensen, eds., *Approaches to Peace.*

Cohen, Raymond (1991). *Negotiating Across Cultures: Communication Obstacles in International Diplomacy.* Washington, D.C.: United States Institute of Peace Press.

——— (1990). *Culture and Conflict in Egyptian-Israeli Relations: A Dialogue of the Deaf.* Bloomington: Indiana University Press.

Cunningham, J. Barton (1984). "Assumptions underlying the use of different types of simulations," *Simulation & Games,* 15 (2): 213-234.

Druckman, Daniel (1973). *Human Factors in International Negotiations.* Beverly Hills, Calif.: Sage Publications.

———, ed. (1977). *Negotiations: Social Psychological Perspectives.* Beverly Hills, Calif.: Sage Publications.

Duke, Richard D. (1974). *Gaming: The Future's Language.* Newbury Park, Calif.: Sage Publications.

——— (1989). "Gaming/simulation: A gestalt communications form." In David Crookall and Danny Saunders, eds., *Communication and Simulation: From Two Fields to One Theme.* Clevedon, England: Multilingual Matters.

Dutton, Jane E., and Stephen A. Stumpf (1991). "Using behavioral simulations to study strategic processes," *Simulation & Games,* 22 (2): 149-173.

Fisher, Glen (1982). *International Negotiation: A Cross-Cultural Perspective.* Yarmouth, Me.: Intercultural Press.

——— (1988). *Mindsets: The Role of Culture and Perception in International Relations.* Yarmouth, Me.: Intercultural Press.

Fisher, Ronald (1990). *The Social Psychology of Intergroup and International Conflict Resolution.* New York: Springer-Verlag.

George, Alexander (forthcoming, spring 1993). *Bridging the Gap: Theory and Practice in Foreign Policy.* Washington, D.C.: United States Institute of Peace Press.

Gilpin, Robert (1981). *War and Change in World Politics.* New York: Cambridge University Press.

Goldberg, Andrew C., Debra Van Opstal, and James H. Barkley, eds. (1990). *Avoiding the Brink: Theory and Practice in Crisis Management.* McLean, Va.: Brassey's.

Guetzkow, Harold, et al. (1963). *Simulation in International Relations: Developments for Research and Teaching.* Englewood Cliffs, N.J.: Prentice-Hall.

Hoffman, Lloyd H., Jr. (1984). "Defense war gaming," *Orbis,* 27 (4): 812-822.

Jervis, Robert (1976). *Perception and Misperception in International Politics.* Princeton, N.J.: Princeton University Press.

Korzenny, Felipe, and Stella Ting-Toomey, eds. (1990). *Communicating for Peace: Diplomacy and Negotiation.* Newbury Park, Calif.: Sage Publications.

Lakos, Amos (1989). *International Negotiation: A Bibliography.* Boulder, Colo.: Westview.

Laue, James H. (forthcoming). "Getting to the table: Preparing for negotiations in deep rooted disputes," *Sociological Practice.*

——— (1991). "Contributions of the emerging field of conflict resolution." In Thompson and Jensen, eds., *Approaches to Peace.* Washington, D.C.: United States Institute of Peace Press.

Laue, James H., Sharon Burd, William Potapchuk, and Miranda Salkoff (1988). "Getting to the table: Three paths," *Mediation Quarterly,* 20 (2): 7-21.

Levy, Jack S. (1989). "The causes of war: A review of theories and evidence." In Philip E. Tetlock, Jo L. Husbands, Robert Jervis, Paul C. Stern, and Charles Tilly, eds., *Behavior, Society and Nuclear War,* vol 1. New York: Oxford University Press.

Mitchell, C. R. (1981). *The Structure of International Conflict.* New York: St. Martin's Press.

Morgenthau, Hans J. (1973). *Politics Among Nations.* 5th ed. New York: Knopf.

Osgood, Charles E. (1980). "The GRIT strategy," *Bulletin of Atomic Scientists,* May, pp. 58-60.

Rohrlich, Paul E. (1987). "Why do we study intercultural communication?" *International Journal of Intercultural Relations,* 11: 123-128.

Saunders, Harold (1985). "We need a larger theory of negotiation: The importance of prenegotiation," *Negotiation Journal,* 1: 249-262.

————— (1990). "An historic challenge to rethink how nations relate." In Vamik Volkan, Demetrios Julies, and Joseph Montville, eds., *The Psychodynamics of International Relationships*, vol. 1: *Concepts and Theories*. Lexington, Mass.: Lexington Books.

Stein, Janice Gross, ed. (1989). *Getting to the Table: The Processes of International Prenegotiation*. Baltimore: Johns Hopkins University Press.

Stein, Kenneth W., and Samuel W. Lewis, with Sheryl J. Brown (1991). *Making Peace Among Arabs and Israelis: Lessons from Fifty Years of Negotiating Experience*. Washington, D.C.: United States Institute of Peace.

Thatcher, Donald C. (1986). "Promoting learning through games and simulations." *Simulation & Games*, 17 (3): 262-273.

Thompson, W. Scott, and Kenneth M. Jensen, with Richard N. Smith and Kimber M. Schraub, eds. (1991). *Approaches to Peace: An Intellectual Map*. Washington, D.C.: United States Institute of Peace Press.

Toth, Ferenc L. (1988a). "Policy exercises: Objectives and design elements," *Simulation & Games*, 19 (3): 235-255.

————— (1988b). "Policy exercises: Procedures and implementations," *Simulation & Games*, 19 (3): 256-276.

Waltz, Kenneth (1959). *Man, the State and War*. New York: Columbia University Press.

————— (1979). *Theory of International Politics*. Reading, Mass.: Addison-Wesley.

Winham, Gilbert R. (1991). "Simulation for teaching and analysis." In Victor A. Kremenyuk, ed., *International Negotiation: Analysis, Approaches, Issues*. San Francisco, Calif.: Josey-Bass Publishers. Pp. 409-423.

Wise, Kenneth L. (1991). *Crisis Management in Foreign Policy: A Guide to Directing Simulations*. Washington, D.C.: Atlantic Council.

Wood, B. H., ed. (1972). *History of Chess*. London: Abbey Library.

Zartman, I. William (1989). "Prenegotiation: Phases and functions." In Stein, ed., *Getting to the Table*.

Zartman, I. William, and Maureen Berman (1982). *The Practical Negotiator*. New Haven, Conn.: Yale University Press.

United States Institute of Peace

The United States Institute of Peace is an independent, nonpartisan federal institution created and funded by Congress to strengthen the nation's capacity to promote the peaceful resolution of international conflict. Established in 1984, the Institute has its origins in the tradition of American statesmanship, which seeks to limit international violence and to achieve a just peace based on freedom and human dignity. The Institute meets its congressional mandate to expand available knowledge about ways to achieve a more peaceful world through an array of programs, including grantmaking, a three-tiered fellowship program, research and studies projects, development of library resources, and a variety of citizen education activities. The Institute is governed by a fifteen-member Board of Directors, including four members ex officio from the executive branch of the federal government and eleven individuals appointed from outside federal service by the President of the United States and confirmed by the Senate.